The buzzards, and other poems

Martin Donisthorpe Armstrong

Nabu Public Domain Reprints:

You are holding a reproduction of an original work published before 1923 that is in the public domain in the United States of America, and possibly other countries. You may freely copy and distribute this work as no entity (individual or corporate) has a copyright on the body of the work. This book may contain prior copyright references, and library stamps (as most of these works were scanned from library copies). These have been scanned and retained as part of the historical artifact.

This book may have occasional imperfections such as missing or blurred pages, poor pictures, errant marks, etc. that were either part of the original artifact, or were introduced by the scanning process. We believe this work is culturally important, and despite the imperfections, have elected to bring it back into print as part of our continuing commitment to the preservation of printed works worldwide. We appreciate your understanding of the imperfections in the preservation process, and hope you enjoy this valuable book.

THE BUZZARDS

Martin Armstrong

THE BUZZARDS
AND OTHER POEMS
BY MARTIN ARMSTRONG

LONDON: MARTIN SECKER

First published, 1921

THE LONDON AND NORWICH PRESS, LIMITED, LONDON AND NORWICH, ENGLAND.

NOTE

MANY of these poems have appeared in *The Athenæum, The British Review, The Century Magazine, The London Mercury,* and *The New Statesman*: and two, "Cowardice" and "Spring in Campania" are reprinted from a former volume published in 1912.

M. A.

CONTENTS

Two Garden Pieces, 11
Trees, 13

The Buzzards, 15
The Thrush, 17
The Kingfisher, 19
The Blackbird, 20
The Bat, 21

The Coming of Green, 23
Rainy August, 25
After the Journey, 26
Spring in Campania, 28
The Hedge, 29
In Lamplight, 30
On London Bridge, 31

Polite Conversation, 33
A Pup's Epitaph, 34
A Little Bird's Epitaph, 35

The Church, 37
Hymn to Ideal Beauty, 39
Funeral at Night, 41
Sleep, 43
La Rose est Morte, 44
Rhapsody, 45
The Cathedral, 46
The Explorers, 47
Going up the Line, 49
Vision, 50
Peace, 51

Portrait of an Old Woman, 52
The Senses, 54

Green, 57
Purple, 58
Grey, 59
White, 60
Three Fragments from " The Merchant from the East " :—
    I. Dyes, 62
    II. Waves in Moonlight, 63
    III. Light, 64
Cowardice, 66
Idolaters, 68
Miss Thompson Goes Shopping, 69
The Wise Man's Song, 77

TWO GARDEN PIECES

I

Birds, whose clear singing reaches
   To furthest corners of these still garden-halls
   Pillared with ancient beeches
   And floored with quiet green
Of smoothly-spreading lawns, where falls
   Sunlight—golden, warm, serene,
   Laid like shining banners in between
     The long boughs' falls:
  O birds, your singing reaches
Mysteriously through the soul's dim halls,
   Troubles its sleep and teaches
      By those pure calls
Dead love, forgotten sweetness, vanished pain,
To rise and hold my hands and clasp my arms;
Till, freed from Time's indignities and harms,
   My dearest steps again
From the grey porch, and we like gods great-hearted,
Our love reborn and the life-long ache departed,
Pace with delight grass walks and sunny reaches,
Regrets and hopes laid-by, wrapt in sereneness
Breathed out from wide aisles of unfading beeches,
   And the long lawn's greenness.

II

   O holy trees,
Green homes of unperturbed tranquillities,
O beeches, thriving in a long content,
Let me behold you and in contemplation
   Drain this refreshment sent

From your pure being, free from domination
Of angers, sorrows, and the long disease
Of hope, the long anxiety of love;
So patiently receiving from above
Sunlight and rain and the changing ministration
Of circling years, and from the deep earth taking
Your needed food; the servants of no strife
   Nor laws of your own making,
But only that divine law which is Life.
Oh, out of your serene abundance give
To our blind poverty the gift that saves,
   That we at length may live:
And afterwards draw beauty from our graves.

TREES

Beautiful trees that in the early morning
Stand up golden in the golden light,
A wonder of peace and colour and airy height,
With curve on lovely curve of boughs adorning
This garden arisen dewy out of the night:

Fair presences, serene and tall, reflecting
Rosy light of evening, gold of dawn,
With wind-enchanted, whispering screen protecting
    This green, close-shorn,
Hidden circle of bird-haunted lawn:

Seeing your lovely springtime and your season
Of bland and tranquil death, my soul delighted
Sings out to yours, while Joy, the spirit's Reason,
Up heights too steep for thought leads on clear-sighted
Till in a sudden flash the eye can capture
Unbroken sight of the endless sea of Being
Where the shadow of self drowns in immortal rapture.

THE BUZZARDS

When evening came and the warm glow grew deeper
And every tree that bordered the green meadows
And in the yellow cornfields every reaper
And every corn-shock stood above their shadows
Flung eastward from their feet in longer measure,
Serenely far there swam in the sunny height
A buzzard and his mate who took their pleasure
Swirling and poising idly in golden light.
On great pied motionless moth-wings borne along,
So effortless and so strong,
Cutting each other's paths, together they glided,
Then wheeled asunder till they soared divided
Two valleys' width (as though it were delight
To part like this, being sure they could unite
So swiftly in their empty, free dominion),
Curved headlong downward, towered up the sunny steep,
Then, with a sudden lift of the one great pinion,
Swung proudly to a curve and from its height
Took half a mile of sunlight in one long sweep.

And we, so small on the swift immense hillside,
Stood tranced, until our souls arose uplifted
On those far-sweeping, wide,
Strong curves of flight,—swayed up and hugely drifted,
Were washed, made strong and beautiful in the tide
Of sun-bathed air. But far beneath, beholden
Through shining deeps of air, the fields were golden
And rosy burned the heather where cornfields ended.

And still those buzzards wheeled, while light withdrew
Out of the vales and to surging slopes ascended,
Till the loftiest-flaming summit died to blue.

THE THRUSH

From the high rampart of the sleepy town
He watched through twigs of bare and blackened elms
Blue January evening settle down
Out of the sky's serene and watery realms,
Mingling with smoke from every darkening home,
And dull the low red roofs, and permeate
The blurred and winding streets, and urge its gloom
Across the lawns of damp and desolate
Long gardens. And on all this humble drift
He saw, built up of gloomy atmosphere,
The presence of the grey cathedral lift
Its gathered towers. But very cold and clear
The unfathomed height of sky. There faintest blues,
Pale violet, paler rose, and ocean-cool
Green beryl gleamed, as streams of many hues
Might meet and swim together in a pool.
But in the westward trees a golden gleam
Deepened and died. And all hung in a dream
    Pure, passionless, and stilled.

Then on a leafless bough the silence thrilled,
Took sudden voice, became a soul upspringing
In a pure untroubled rapture of clear singing:
And the cool furled bud of evening suddenly flowering
Burst to an odorous bloom, and the silver-showering
Fountain-basin of Quietness brimmed over,
And Mortal Life embraced her spirit lover.

But the long former space of evening hush
Sank beyond thought, and that divine unfolding
Became eternity in the heart.
                    O thrush,
On the topmost bough your bill and throat upholding:
O small, smooth-feathered body, infinite Voice;
You pipe from blackening boughs to the faded sky
Not only utterance of your own small joys,
    Child of immensity!·
O harp from which the winds draw harmony!
Summer of roses in the seed's small kernel!
You voice the indrawn breath of life, the eternal,
Brooding upon itself in ecstasy,
Till time and space are lost in golden weather,
And dead loves rise again and sing together,
And the loves unborn with tender life are stirred
    At the summons of a bird.
But he upon the city walls enchanted,
A dark, unmoving shade, forgetful, lone
Among dark tree-trunks, while the bird descanted,
Was caught into the song till light was flown.

THE KINGFISHER

Under the bank, close-shaded from the sun;
    By winter freshets spun,
Dry, tangled wreckage hung above the shallows
    In the bare roots of the sallows,
And underneath in cool twilight the stream
    Lay calmed to a brown dream.

Then with the leap and flash of a swift blue flame
    Out from the dusk he came
And the heart and the breath stood still with delight and wonder
    While in the water under
Shot, swift as he, a streak of blue and green
    From unseen to unseen.

O Wonder, leaping with sudden flash of wings
    From the litter of common things,
Shine on the inward eye till the soul leaps higher
    On the surge of a great desire
And high in the dim-lit hall of earthly years
    Another lamp appears.

THE BLACKBIRD

Evening over fields of cloud
   In sombre beauty came,
Washing the slumbering trees with mist
   And the tall spires with flame.

Then from one of the still trees
   Like drops that run along
The glossy faces of green leaves,
   Fell a blackbird's song:

And Memory opened dreaming eyes
   And the pale ghosts stirred,
And heaven and earth went down before
   The soft note of a bird.

For as the hidden blackbird spoke
   Out of the leafy tree,
One long and shining wave-crest broke
   Along a secret sea.

THE BAT

After the sun is gone,
   And the air grows chill
And quiet, pure and wan
   From hill to hill,
And the wide space of the lane
   From side to side
Is full of the pale green water of eventide,

And a blurring mist of blue
   Gathers and floods
Under the dim close-woven thatch of the woods,
   So dim, so closely-twigged,
     So screened from view
   That the sunset's furrowed flame
     Can scarce show through:

Then in some grey barn
   From cobwebbed beam
A bat will drop, to flit
   In the fading gleam—
A flickering silhouette
   Like a headless bird,
Flapping softly, diving
   On wings unstirred,
Or like a torn black rag
   Poised flutteringly,
Or whirled in frantic loops
   Too quick to see.

But when from dusk-blue woods,
   From misty park,
Out of dim-watered ditches,
   Wells the dark,

Then all seen things dissolve
  To ghosts . . . to naught . . .
Emptiness haunted by a thing distraught—
  A blind, distracted flight,
    Bewildered, lost,
  And the thin, pale cry in the night
    Of a bloodless ghost.

THE COMING OF GREEN

Here like flame and there like water leaping
Green life breaks out again—in sunlight gleaming
Small bright emerald flames through grey twigs
    creeping,
Little freshets of leafage shyly streaming
Among dark tangles. And sunlight grows serener
Daily, and wider extends the leafy awning,
And the green undying lawn below grows greener—
Greener and lovelier with lights and shadows
    dawning
Alternate, many-toned, born of the trooping
Of clouds o'er sun. Assembled Planes are bending
Long festoons high-hung and heavily-drooping
From domes of luminous greenness. Willows are
    sending
Their fountains live and many-shafted towering
Skyward, and lazily backward coolly showering.

Like tongues of flame, like water showering,
    dripping,
Green life slides down the branch, from bushes
    shaking
A verdant dew, or, out on a long curve slipping,
At the far extreme to a shivering soft foam break-
    ing.

A spring in the desert, a fire in the darkness
    leaping,
Greenness comes, transparently roofing and walling
Garden ways with an indolent downward-sweeping,
Or mounded high, . . . aspiring, . . . airily fall-
    ing,

Or leaning fan over fan. A green and golden
Lucid cave enfolds us, cunningly vaulted,
With delicate-screened high chambers to embolden
Birds to flutter and sing or nest exalted
In swaying sanctuaries, and the Lime-tree's clustering
Flowers to blow that the leafy ways be fragrant.

A dancing flood, a wild fire strengthening, mustering,
Over the gardens the young green life runs vagrant.

RAINY AUGUST

Here all day long the sound of falling rain
Ripples among green boughs and softly hisses
    Upon smooth lawns and kisses
The roses full of crystal drops that grow
Until a petal bends and the bright drops flow
From petal to petal onto the leaves below:

And every night is hushed with the sigh of rain
    That never beats the pane
So straight it falls. For hours the unbroken sighing
Of rainfall fills dark bedrooms, till the flying
    Wings of a sudden breeze
Spill showers of pattering raindrops out of the trees
    And trouble a thousand leaves,
Or a flooded gutter sheds from the high eaves
    A rhythmic, muted, slow,
Musical dropping into the pool below.

Yet sometimes, ere the afternoon is done,
    A smile of unlooked-for sun
Gilds a bough, then mellows and embraces
Other boughs, then fires the verdant spaces
Of rain-soaked lawn, then, momently richer glowing,
Spreads, far-seen through burning tree-trunks, throwing
A splendour across far hills for miles and miles.

    So have I seen the face
    Of one who seldom smiles
    Take on a sudden grace,
    A sudden youthful fairness
    More lovely for its rareness.

AFTER THE JOURNEY

Between red firelight and yellow lamplight seated
With legs sprawled idly to the rosy blaze
In a warm delightful sleepiness I gaze,
Seeing in the mirror's watery light repeated
Glossy curtains and ceiling flushed to yellow
And, gleaming on their background blurred and mellow,
Three shapes :—a vase from Venice, frail and pure
As a bubble changed to ice, a green-glazed jar
Gilded with flakes of candlelight that star
Its rounded flank, and, third, a porcelain lady
Shrinking half-naked, impudently demure.
Thinking of nothing, desiring nothing, secure
From toil, except to raise a wineglass mouthward,
I blandly dream, until the scene grows shady,
Melts . . . swims together . . . opens wide and stormy,
And the great blue downs rise grandly up before me,
A barren wall receding swiftly southward
And far behind us into broad plains merging.
But as the train whirls on, through smoke-wreaths loom
Their ramparts, huge and huger grown, converging
Until their swollen flanks close in and, surging
Enormous in the window-space, consume
The last small glimpse of sky. And then unfold
Parkland and woodland, tawny and green and gold :—

Like sudden fire above the grassy reaches
The orange splendour of autumnal beeches
With level-curving boughs like flames blown forward:
And up the rising slopes, as waves run shoreward,
The russet woodlands climbing clefts and valleys.
Rooks wheel, and there a straggling patch of cover
Among bare thorns and hazel-bushes rallies
A flock of misty birches freckled over
With little amber leaves. Here, weed-encrusted,
A willow-circled water richly glasses
Gold-dropping boughs: a group of elms gold-dusted
Muffles a farm, and like a vision passes
The yellow rain of larches. Smoke goes trailing
Over the woods and fields. The light is failing.
Then sunset, gloaming, darkness, and the train's
Roaring through country stations down the plains.

SPRING IN CAMPANIA

Now that in vineyard and wood awakens the sleeper,
   And pallid aconite-flames break out in the fuel
Of mouldering leafage; now that the sky grown deeper
   Blossoms to hyacinth-blue, and the sea is a jewel,
And wandering rain the drouth of the vine-stems eases,
   And butterfly-like on the bough the blossom uncloses;
Visions of Dryads with hair caught up on the breezes
   (Sun-hued hair and breasts like the petals of roses),
Swim on the ether, and Oreads pale as sea-water
   Circle in fluttering green, pink-fringed like flowers.
Loud-singing bees go questing the waxen mortar
To fashion their six-walled cells that a hundred bowers
Shall plenish with nectar. Voices of reed-pipes waken
   Under the hills, where, hid in some ferny antre,
Satyrs mimic the birds. The air is shaken
   With laughter of working peasants and songs and banter:
For now they prune the olives and train the vine-shoots,
   Watching the buds and blades—taught once by Apollo
How in the blade springs the bread, in the grape-bud the wine shoots,
   And after the pruning the young wood sprouts from the hollow.

THE HEDGE

All through the long drought of summer weather
    This deep, high-branching hedge,
So cool and sombre along the field's long edge,
Shed reposeful gloom when all was glowing
And a cooling smell of leaves and green things
    growing:
And the many kinds of trees so thronged together,
Black-stemmed hawthorns, beech-boughs of bright
    feather,
Cherries with lacquered bark and slender birches
    Where the sky linnet perches,
And silver-wanded rowans—all were seen
Of one unbroken shade of humble green.

And so through autumntide. But when I came
Over the fields one morning in October,
    That thicket, once so sober,
Had leapt into a festival of flame.
Scarlet burned the rowans and the cherries
Flared to the sky; on the pied hawthorn-bushes
    Clustered the crimson berries
    That feed the missel-thrushes,
And the silver shafts of birches rose and shattered
To fountains of golden leaves against the blue,
And beech-leaves tawny and orange like sunlight
    minted
Rustled along a tapering bough that hinted
Of busy squirrels hurrying out of view,
And all the path beneath the hedge was scattered
With fallen and drifted leafage of lovely hue.

IN LAMPLIGHT

Now that the chill October day is declining,
Pull the blinds, draw each voluminous curtain,
Till the room is full of gloom and of the uncertain
Gleams of firelight on polished edges shining.
Then bring the rosy lamp to its wonted station
On the dark-gleaming table. In that soft splendour
Well-known things of the room, grown deep and tender,
Gather round, a mysterious congregation:
Pallid sheen of the silver, the bright brass fender,
The wine-red pool of carpet, the bowl of roses,
Lustrous-hearted, crimsons and purples looming
From dusky rugs and curtains. Nothing discloses
The unseen walls, but the broken, richly-glooming
Gold of frames and opulent wells of mingling
Dim colours gathered in darkened mirrors. And breaking
The dreamlike spell, and out of your deep chair moving
You go, perhaps, to the shelves and, slowly singling
Some old rich-blazoned book, return. But the gleaming
Spells close round you again and you fall to dreaming,
Eyes grown dim, the book on your lap unheeded.

ON LONDON BRIDGE

In dull December weather
When the town is brimmed with mist,
Evening comes showering from the sky
In a rain of amethyst:

Evening descends upon the town
Like the soft bloom on a grape
Till the buildings ranked and piled become
One many-towered shape

Modelled and moulded out of light,
Soft-coloured light that glows
On the eastward sides like violet
And westward like the rose:

And all along the river-bank
Twilight so blue descends
That it hides where the windowed walls begin
And where the water ends:

And in the hollow beneath the bridge
Dim grows the air, until
Only a steel-blue ripple gleams
And the water's breath breathes chill.

POLITE CONVERSATION

I loafed about the lawn in Russell Square
   While spring was busy there,
When lo, a Dryad from a chestnut-tree
   Poked out her head at me
And put her fingers to her nose and sneered,
   Then crowed and disappeared.
Soon came a pattering in the leaves like rain
   And out she popped again.
"I really think you rather rude," I said.
   She shook a solemn head
And spoke :—"I simply can't behave, I fear,
   At this time of the year."
"Of course," I said. Then she, with sidelong
   glance :—
   "Have you, by any chance,
The time upon you?" "Time? It's ten past
   four."
   "Thank you. But what a bore."
"Why, what the deuce have you to do with
   time?"
   "The Dryad in that lime
Has asked me to a Musical At-Home.
   'Be sure,' she said, 'you come.'
And now I've only half-an-hour or less
   To do my hair and dress.
Good-bye. I fear you thought me indiscreet?"
   Said I :—"Don't mention it."
She smiled :—"I am so glad you understand."
   And, waving one small hand,
She dived again into the shaking tree
   And I went home to tea.

A PUP'S EPITAPH

Punch was a mongrel pup
   Short-haired and brown,
His tail was always up,
   His muzzle down :

Whom once a motor-van
   Took by surprise
And flattened out, poor man,
   And here he lies.

A LITTLE BIRD'S EPITAPH

Here lies a little bird :
   Once all day long
Through Martha's house was heard
   His rippled song.

Tread lightly where he lies
   Beneath this stone,
With nerveless wings, closed eyes,
   And sweet voice gone.

THE CHURCH

1

That wide expanse of pavement unencumbered,
Fenced with pillar and calm arch upholding
Windows and the high roof's painted moulding
Where morning light of centuries had slumbered,
That airy church, harmonious with the unnumbered
Voices of silence, seemed to be designed
Not to display a vision of the mind
Like other buildings; rather to enclose
Pure Space, a spirit undefined and free,
Moving as beauty, soothing as repose:
For here cool-lighted Space was felt to be
A living presence, a divinity.

2

Then on the frozen beauty of that spell,
(As drops of rosy wine, poured one by one
Into a glass of water, melt and run
Tingeing the clear) the bright note of a bell
And then another and another fell
And one that spoke with a deep and golden tone:
Shedding a coloured music, a wavering drone
Rippling about the arches, stealthily coming
Along the silence, expanding curved and round,
Washing the air with a rich, mysterious humming,
Brimming windows and walls to the furthest bound
With a mellow brightness, a rosy glow of sound.

3

And still that pool of sound would gleam and shake
As each bell dropped its jewel through the gloom
From the tenor's sharp bright clang to the bass's boom
That shed upon the mist its burning flake,
Till the pealing ended suddenly, and that lake
Of music thinned, evaporated, faded,
To eddy away along the hollow shaded
Aisles and among the dusty beams to fly,
In curling wisps of resonance dying down,
Ebbing, faltering, drifting far and high,
A trembling echo, a faint vibrating tone,
And the muted memory when the note is gone.

4

But in the wake of those departed voices
Silence came welling back along the nave
And empty Space again grew cool and grave
Washed of the colours of those mingled noises,
Crossed only by the evening light that poises
On wall and column and the wide floor-spaces,
And the shadows lengthened from their hiding-places.
Then from the transept moved in slow progression
Bright shapes that crossed with a gliding, coloured weft
The warp of slim grey pillars; whose procession,
Ascending the wide altar-stair, was cleft
And curled asunder to the right and left.

HYMN TO THE IDEAL BEAUTY

Eternal Beauty, phœnix never-dying,
Consumed for ever in thine eternal fire
And ever from the smouldering ashes flying
Bright and refreshed and plumed to circle higher,
Stronger than eagle, swifter than the swallow,
More lovely than the peacock, sweeter-throated
Than moon-charmed nightingale, thy fires have
    floated
Through the dreams of endless generations
Who stir in sleep and wake and rise to follow
That fleeting glimpse of high imaginations,
Restless, unsatisfied : for we, frail mortals,
How can we grasp the infinite, or bind
Her fluttering wings, although the eager mind
Conceive high-vaulted halls and sculptured portals
And sunlit towers to lure her for a day,
Set a snare of music to enfold her,
Weave a web of words across her way,
    Spread a net to hold her
Of colours lovelier than the richest petal
Or delicate scheme of dance and song and rhyme,
Staying her flight, bewitching her to settle
A moment on the withering boughs of time.
But ah, with the first cool touch of the dawn
    to-morrow
She stirs and spreads her dewy wings to fly,
And wise men gaze ahead and banish sorrow
Knowing that if she linger she must die.
For we can keep her only if we lose her,
And only he that patiently pursues her
Spies her again, a swift light in the sky,

    And sees the dim world brighten
And feels her radiance through his dark soul
    lighten,
And seeks and finds her where she flies to cover,
But never shall he clasp her as a lover.

O milk-white swan from the dark cloud careening,
Ecstasy unfulfilled, frustrated rest,
Bright truth whereof we strain to glimpse a
    meaning,
You come at the call of our undying quest
Out of the darkness, as from a window, leaning
With pure delicious profile, carven shoulder,
Bright arm and ivory contour of a breast,
Leaning towards us : but when we, grown bolder,
Stretch eager arms, alas, the dream has faded,
Gone the white body, the pure face departed,
Leaving us in the darkness empty-hearted
And all our noble enterprise unaided.

FUNERAL AT NIGHT

Down the dark street, so cavernous and so bare,
So far from the stars, so shut from the open air,
So narrowly walled between the frowning height
Of palaces, so dank in the autumn chills,
There came a stir of turbulent red light
And a thin, lamenting music in broken thrills.
Then throngs of brandished torches swung in sight,
    Streaming, smoking torches,
    Conjuring vaults and porches
To leap from the dark in wild and fitful flashes
    And carving crimson gashes
On shutters and blank walls. O tragic starkness
Of flapping flames! O terrible shrillness
Of blown fifes, breaking on the darkness,
    Piercing through the stillness!
O dim, mysterious, hooded multitude bearing
The huge draped coffin through the smoke and
    flaring
Of tawny, shaken flames! Is death so fearful,
A thing of fire and darkness and the tearful
Shrieking of fifes, a thing of terror dreamed
In madness? Round them, thick and choking,
    steamed
A stench of unseen dust and the sick fume
Of incense and burnt grease, that seemed to be
Very miasma of mortality.

They passed in chaos of blown fire and gloom
And shuffled feet, into the dark square turning.
There wide stone steps came flickering into sight
And they heaved the huge draped coffin up the
    flight

Into the cavern of a great church bright
With the misty stars of a hundred candles burning.

And down the deep street returning stealthily
Came softly-whispering silence like a sea,
And darkness swaddled in her sable shroud.
And there, between the roofs, low-hung in misty
    air
The crescent moon was leaning slim and fair
As Aphrodite on a couch of cloud.

SLEEP

Into the crystal-green waters of sleep
    Sink him deep and deep,
Down the sheer walls of water wavering slow
    As a dead leaf from the bough,
Falling, dropping away from sight and sound
    Down into deeps profound:
Down and down until the twilight-green
    Is changed to a twilight-blue
That blurs the memory of all things seen
And draws a screen that no clear voice breaks through:
Floating with limbs relaxed and the wandering mind
    Effortless, dumb, and blind,
And the senses charmed by the gradual ebb and flow
    Of curling tides that go
Mixing the cooler waters with the warm
    Far from all wind and storm.
Then from the shadowy rocks of those low streams
    Gather the glimmering dreams
To glide with wafted fin and gleaming scale
    Or set a pearly sail
To catch the tide and circle round his head
Building bright canopies above his bed
Until he lapse into profoundest sleep
    Even for dreams too deep.
    Down, down, and down,
Where memory, thought, and every sense must drown
And tired body and mind lie cradled free
In the cool darkness of nonentity.

LA ROSE EST MORTE . . .

A lady slumbers here,
  So wise, so noble,
That when the times turned sere
  She'd never trouble,

But, seeing how earthward-shed
  Each petal goes,
She'd sing :—" The rose is dead,
  Long live the rose."

RHAPSODY

As when trees are shrouded in December
Men recall the perfumes of the flower-time,
So we sing a life we half remember :—
How we heard in some primeval shower-time
Liquid song of rain upon blue rivers :
Dreamed on isles in windless oceans planted
Where a dim green twilight bird-enchanted
Under domes of drooping leafage quivers :
How we climbed, on many a hidden planet,
Eagle-heights stirred by a starry breeze :
Watched by coffined kings in tombs of granite
Where the darkness hangs like boughs of trees,
Glimpsing in the reddening light of torches
Ghosts of sombre vaults and looming porches,
Cyclopean faces, giant knees :
How we anchored in a violet haven,
Seeking under light of unknown stars
Mountains paler than the moonlight, graven
Into shapes of pinnacles and scars :
Where our boat set all the lilies swinging
Sailed up rivers hushed and leafy-arboured
And, in caves of hanging blossom harboured,
Heard the sound of an immortal singing.

As when breathed upon, the ashen ember
Blossoms into fire again and fades,
So bright June's flame up through our December
And at random whiles we half remember
Sudden gusts of an immortal singing,
Ancient visions of remote crusades.

THE CATHEDRAL

Here dreams of men long dead,
Beautiful dreams, sublime imagining,
Clear aspirations that too often wing
Straight to the infinite from the heart and leave
No human record (being too divine,
Too flamelike for the dreamer to enshrine
In mortal shape)—here such as these receive
An earthly form in tall, serene arcades,
Slim shafts that leap to meet among the shades
Of misty vaults, clustering and fretted spires
Of high tomb-canopies, the lustrous fires
Of sun-illumined windows, and these towers,
    With ivory turrets crowned,
Uplifted joyfully among the powers
Of sunlight and clean winds that wash them round
With golden atmosphere. And from their tops
Isled in the air, the jackdaws launch away
Into the lake of sunlight, soar and sway
In happy flight that curves and lifts and drops.
And the twelve gilded vanes stand clear and high,
    So steeply far away,
Like little tongues of flame against blue sky.

THE EXPLORERS

We are those wandering souls that never rest:
No ancient loves can bind us, for the zest
And hunger of the eternal in us burn,
Driving us to adventure and to spurn
Ease and the humble joys within our ken
In the narrow earthly heavens of little men :—
Hunger for great experience, wisdom deep
Of nature and ourselves, those truths that leap
Flamelike to greet the faithful stress of soul
That forges on, seeking the glittering pole
Through pain and terror and heart's agony
And many a windy battle on the sea.

Sunsets chaotic, fierce, and beautiful
Fire the long furrow of our cleaving hull
And gild the coasts with wild and changing lights
Still ominous of elemental fights.
And the known coasts fall behind; the plunging ship
Leaps through untravelled seas. And, lo, the grip
About our hearts of a sudden delighted fear
As the starry wonders glimmer and grow clear
Nightly, to nourish that unsated will
That goads us ever on to struggle still
On weltering decks in the roaring of ripped sails,
With maniac seas and screaming winds and the flails
Of lashing rain, in the clatter of hurled spray,
Through nights moonless and starless, through long day

Of twilight windless till at evenfall
Thunder and lightning usher in the squall.

The loudest storms die down and cease to be,
But nourished with their strength and laughter we,
Unbeaten wrestlers, ever onward roll
With warm, sea-freshened body and laughing soul,
Still eager for whatever shall befall;
And still, like lion-tamers, proudly call
New terrors and wonders forth from the unknown:
Gathering from toil and terrors overthrown,
From keen adventure and unabashed endeavour
The ambrosial food that keeps us young for ever;
Seeking new worlds until our souls shall be
Wide as the frontiers of divinity.

GOING UP THE LINE

O consolation and refreshment breathed
From the young Spring with apple-blossom
    wreathed,
    Whose certain coming blesses
All life with token of immortality,
And from the ripe beauty and human tendernesses
And reconcilement and tranquillity
Which are the spirit of all things grown old.
    For now that I have seen
The curd-white hawthorn once again
    Break out on the new green,
And through the iron gates in the long blank wall
    Have viewed across a screen
Of rosy apple-blossom the grey spire
And low red roofs and humble chimney-stacks,
And stood in spacious courtyards of old farms,
And heard green virgin wheat sing to the breeze,
And the drone of ancient worship rise and fall
In the dark church, and talked with simple folk
Of farm and village, dwelling near the earth,
Among earth's ancient elemental things:
    I can with heart made bold
Go back into the ways of ruin and death
With step unflagging and with quiet breath,
For drawn from the hidden Spirit's deepest well
I carry in my soul a power to quell
    All ills and terrors such as these can hold.

A VISION

In a paradise I lie of leaves and flowers:
Long boughs hang from above in luminous showers:
    Rose-scented the warm air.
A hidden water mingles its lisping sound
With the sultry music of bees, and the sense is
    drowned
In a pool of warm delight. But as it drowses
Deep and to outward things serenely closes,
Some freak of the uncharted mind lays bare . . .
No richer summer, deeper-hearted roses,
But greyness, rain, and ruin, and in the air
A flying sorrow as some forlorn shell whines
From silence into silence over the still
Brown deserts of torn earth, and the charred
    stains
Of shell-bursts, and the scrawled unending lines
Of battered trench where, blackening in the rains,
The dead lie out upon the naked hill.

PEACE

Here in this slough our lives grow stale and old,
The body soiled and clogged, the soul consumed
In fear and doubt and memories, being sold
Into the bondage of stagnation. Plumed
For rapturous flight, our wings are snared in mazes
Of palsying thought, and, all brave dreams departed,-
We sit in peace, wise-eyed and empty-hearted,
Like solemn parrots chattering well-learned phrases.

    Show me the deed that must be done,
    The perfect deed, and I will run,
    Though fire and murder flood the dark,
    Singing and swift upon the mark
    As the shell sings from the gun.
    For soul desires not death or life
    But only clean immortal strife,
    The white-hot act that sears away
    Canker of an outworn day,
    Devours the past and all its trash
    And forges new worlds in a flash.

PORTRAIT OF AN OLD WOMAN

1

In the old house beside the long sea-sands
With white-frilled cap and the veined and bony hands
And shoulders hunched beneath the load of years
She sits alone, quite still as though she hears
A distant step: the pale eyes fixed, almost
With the patient, keen expectancy of blindness,
Waiting, it seems, for something, for some frail ghost,
Some gentle ghost of the distant girlhood days.
But if you speak she'll stir herself and raise
Blue eyes grown soft with a certain wistful kindness
And just that touch of wonder in the glance
As though recalled out of the dim expanse
Of dreams. And then, when all the talk is over,
Her gaze ebbs back to the vagueness of long waiting.
Waiting? Is it not rather than under cover
Of age, in the absence of hoping, scheming, hating,
Desires, or cares, she sits in mere repose
Of quietude, forgetfulness, the freeing
Of human bonds, in a pure untroubled being,—
A candle burning with clear unwavering beam:
Since nothing remains for which she could be waiting
But the coming of the long sleep that knows no dream.

2

   This is she
Whom Edmund loved. Leaving the bitter sea
He found her in a yellow-sanded grove
Among sea-loving flowers and the salt sea-breezes:
  And as a fever seizes
And tames a man, so sudden fever of love
Took Edmund, vanquished, maddened him, and drove
To leave his mates and follow her to her home.
  And every day he'd come
To beg a little mercy of her coldness,
Until, as days went by, a gradual boldness
Made her more kind and she would come to nestle
In those bronzed arms that seemed more fit to wrestle
With pirates than to cradle that wild bird.
And, cuddled there, if she rebelled or stirred
He'd clinch her fast, and his rough lips would follow
  The throat's firm slope, to seek
And linger in the soft delicious hollow
Where the neck's warm ivory curves to the smooth cheek.

THE SENSES

    Lo, as a garden-wandering bee,
The soul seeks out her immortality
From all the growths and blossoms manifold
    Which in this life men hold
As things material: plying busy rounds
From the world's odours, sights, and sounds
    To fill her honeyed stores :—

From the perfume acrid-sweet of dead leaves
    burning
When autumn sunsets into dusk are turning:
    From the breath of damp stone floors
And paraffin pervading the cool porches
    And aisles of village churches:
From the tepid, flat, mechanic exhalations
    Of comfortless tube stations:
From woody savours stirred when children wrench
Tufts out of deep moss beds; from the subtle
    stench
Of bad cigars and household slops, begetting
    Delighted memory
Of sunny towns in France and Italy:
From the stronger, tawnier stink of dust and
    sweat
And camel-dung which haunts the glaring East,
And the heavy, sweet, heart-piercing odours
    breathed
From pale large lilies and narcissus wreathed
    Round some dear head deceased.

Such smells as these: and of the sights :—
    The gleam on blue May nights

Of the young moon in high ancestral boughs
    Among the scant young leaves;
And in the wake of the moving ploughs
The shining earth that, as the straight share
    cleaves,
Turns flowingly over: and the half-seen sweep
Of the high circles and the looming hollow
Of the dark opera-house, where through the leap
And lapse of the music unseen hundreds follow
    The curtain's slow ascent:
And the rosy apple-blossom on the bent
And knotted bough, against the blue of heaven:
    And the sudden rainbows riven
By the salt breeze from the billows many-leaping
In the sunny Mediterranean.
                   And of things heard:—
The cooling whisper of summer breezes sweeping
The grey-green barley-fields: and the echoes
    stirred
By music interwoven in some dim-lighted
Cavernous cathedral: and the eighteen-pounders'
Buoyant drumbeats and hisses and whoops united
In a hurricane barrage; and the clear laughter
    and shouting
Of girls in old green gardens playing rounders:
    And the ripple of fountains spouting
On marble nymphs and dolphins drenched and
    cool
    To the sun-splashed fountain-pool
Where golden in the Tuscan sun
    The age-worn palace sleeps.

But deep in all the immortal spirit leaps
Unquenchably, the imperishable one,

To whom, through all this multiplicity
Of scattered universes, longingly
The soul, world-wandering mendicant, upreaches
Imploring hands, and as an alms beseeches
The humble coin which buys that one small
    treasure
        Beyond all earthly measure.

GREEN

While August burns on dusty roads and fields
    I lie beneath green shields
Of coolest shade from a chestnut's airy dome:
And I slowly leave my idle body and roam
    Up through the luminous deep home
Of soft green leaves, move flowingly between
Each motionless light-hung fan, from screen to screen
    Of filtered shadow and light;
From peaceful height ascending to peaceful height
    Where the very air is green.

    But when I have retraced
The lowly journey to our human air,
Who knows what unimagined shores I paced
Or the timeless seasons of my sojourn there.

PURPLE

    Deep, deep is the night,
Brooding, cavernous, beautiful, wide.
    Woods on the blue hillside
Show but as blurs in the gloom more deeply
    glooming,
And the long, familiar barn, so bland in the light,
Is grown phantasmal, a huge shape dimly looming,
A yawning wave upreared to overwhelm
    Us that cower and wonder
    In the heavy shade thereunder,
Dwindled to dwarfs in the midnight's purple
    realm.

GREY

Grey of the twilight, come,
Spread those wide wings above our meadows: bring
Coolness and mist: make dumb
The jarring noise of day, and gently ring
Our woods and ponds with dimness: take away
All busy stir, but let the grey owl sway
Noiselessly over the bough like a little ghost:
And let the cricket in the dark hedge sing
His withered note: and, O Immortal Host,
Welcome this traveller to your drowsy hall
And, standing at the porch, speechless and tall,
Close the great doors, shut out the world, and shed
Your benediction on this drooping head.

WHITE

Lovely through grass the white narcissus reaches
    And lovelier between the trees
The snowy sprinkled mask of anemones
Drifted about the roots of leafless beeches,
So frail in the wind, so delicately petalled
Each seems a small white moth on the twin leaves settled,
Ready to fly at the first light touch of the breeze.

But not the joy of lovely things awaking
    Nor mists of green that creep
Through hedge and copse, nor windflower airily shaking,
Can charm our grief or pleasure the eyes that weep
    Or the dull heart's aching
For the loveliest thing of all fallen asleep.

Search all the gardens, scour the woods and meadows
For pale narcissus, snowdrop, hyacinth,
Crocus and daffodil, to strew the plinth
Of Helen's tomb. And if among the shadows
The white sweet-scented violets yet unfold,
    Hidden in leafy mould,
O bring them too to fade among the rest,
    Where she lies deep and cold.
So that of these, the blooms she loved the best,
Spring's first pure harvest, Death shall not have power
    To rob her of a flower.

But lovely Spring, that leaf by leaf increases
    And scented bloom by bloom,
Brings naught to us for whom all beauty ceases
Under the new-turned mould of Helen's tomb:
For what are flowers to us and what are leaves
    Or blossoms' haunting breath,
But undisguising garlands slow Earth weaves
Before the cold and hollow face of Death.

THREE FRAGMENTS FROM
"THE MERCHANT FROM THE EAST"

I
DYES

My dyeing-vats and looms are in Bagdad
And many a thriving warehouse bears my name
Broadcast about the world—in rich Damascus,
Aleppo, and along the wharves of Cairo,
And, far beyond the Caspian and the mountains,
In Samarkand, Byzantium, Syracuse,
Glittering Amalfi, Cordova and Venice
And Ypres—I touch them all and twenty more,
East, west, flung over lands that roll like seas
And seas that roll like mountains. But I come
Out of the sun's red heart, out of the East,
The well of the world's colour; yes, I bring you
The colour of the East, a lustrous banquet
For eye and soul that sits behind the eye.
I traffic with the sun, barter with him
For all his scale of colours:—ringing sharps
Of scarlet, blue and orange; rich concords
Of mellow flats, deep-rosed or golden-noted
Or murmuring evening-hushed, soft-muted down
To warm and dusky violet. Outside,
Four boys of mine wait with two camel-loads
Of silk: great portly bales of rich brocades,
Smooth lawns, soft veils, sleek velvets of a lustre
And gorgeousness to daze the eyes of kings.

II
WAVES IN MOONLIGHT

A memory like a swallow from the south
Comes fluttering up, of how last year at midnight
I walked the ramparts there, and far below,
Remote as earth beheld out of a star,
The sea hissed softly like a song-charmed snake
And like a moving snake its golden scales
Gleamed dark beneath the moon. Long time I
    leaned
And watched the moonlight damascene the waves
With silver ferns and wavering tongues of light,
Dusking the long wave-hollows, burnishing
The smallest ripple-veins like network cast
On the great lustrous petal of the spent wave
That curved its golden crescent up the shore.

III
Light

O golden light of Love, exhaustless deep:
As the advancing ocean whelms the small
Innumerable pools beneath the rocks
Into assuaging oneness, thou dost brim
The souls of weary men, till shining peace
Serene their aching hearts and lift them up
Out of themselves into the deathless height
Of undivided loveliness. From thee
The nobler life unfolds, the miracle
Comes to fulfilment, and the far-flung sea,
No more a desolation, leaps and burns
With lustrous life, as though the face of Death
Should suddenly grow radiant with desire.
For the fountains of pure light are now unsealed
And poured like a great compassion out of heaven
Upon the waters, and all the air is filled
With the rosy light of Love's own atmosphere.
So nevermore the ocean's voice shall seem
An empty sighing, but the sound of peace
Above the troublous ways of growing life,
Smoothing, atoning, weaving days and years
And life and death into one golden sequence.
This is the reconcilement of the East,
The blossom of resurgent dawns, that links
The one to all, the vision to the clay,
Service of man to the proud soul's secrecy.
Therefore this peace, no peace that comes like sleep,
Dances within us as a quenchless flame,
A living spirit, a transcendent power,
Purging, transmuting all to its own substance . . .

See, like a withered rose the day droops down
Behind the sea, and draws old griefs and fears
Down with it to the abysmal resting-place
Of things forgotten : but the yellow moon
Ascending eastward honeys all the mists
And turns the pools and meres to quicksilver,—
Pale, trembling fires upon the wasted plain.

COWARDICE

The king cried "Bring me colour, the heart's wine ;
   Open my treasuries," he cried, " and heap
Autumnal rubies, emeralds that shine
   Like sunlit seas, and sapphires dark and deep

" As nights of summer, and the shattered glow
   Of irised opals. Bring me sanguine grapes
And tawny-hearted peaches, figs that show
   The purpled pulp, and nectarous plums whose shapes

" Hang down like drops of amber. Fill the urns
   And crystal flagons with clear essences
And glutinous syrups : scatter soft-plumed ferns
   And flowers with crimson throats or cavities

" Cupped with sea-blue, and sunset dahlias,
   And sunflowers round whose fulgent disc are curled
Tongues of gold flame, like the ethereal blaze
   That forged the substance of the teeming world."

They brought him jewels from the treasuries
   And poured them forth before him—sapphires blue
As southern nights, rubies, chalcedonies,
   And fiery opals. Slaves in order due

Bore pyramids of fruit in golden bowls,
   Or heaped on shining salvers : others poured
Rich wines and syrups ; others set on poles
   Torches of frankincense that shed abroad

A curling fragrance down the corridors.
   Flowers wreathed the beams and porches,
     showering
From marble balconies, until the floors
Were drifted deep with petals. And the King

Sat in the midst and let the jewels stream
   Between his fingers, till, in that domain
Utopian, Truth and Fear became a dream
   And he took comfort to his heart again.

IDOLATERS

O slaves of symbols, still aghast
   When symbols of your hopes decay;
Idolaters, who fear to cast
   The serpent's empty slough away;

Behold the Spirit, tameless, fleet,
   Ever to greater mansions move,
And learn at each new death to greet
   The unimprisonment of Love—

Love, sacred, amaranthine rose,
   Whose boughs aspiring to the skies
Shake off dead beauties, to enclose
   The wide domains of Paradise.

MISS THOMPSON GOES SHOPPING
(For J. I. A.)

In her lone cottage on the downs, *Miss Thompson at Home.*
With winds and blizzards and great crowns
Of shining cloud, with wheeling plover
And short grass sweet with the small white clover,
Miss Thompson lived, correct and meek,
A lonely spinster, and every week
On market-day she used to go
Into the little town below,
Tucked in the great downs' hollow bowl
Like pebbles gathered in a shoal.

So, having washed her plates and cup *She goes a-Marketing.*
And banked the kitchen-fire up,
Miss Thompson slipped upstairs and dressed,
Put on her black (her second best),
The bonnet trimmed with rusty plush,
Peeped in the glass with simpering blush,
From camphor-smelling cupboard took
Her thicker jacket off the hook
Because the day might turn to cold.
Then, ready, slipped downstairs and rolled
The hearthrug back: then searched about,
Found her basket, ventured out,
Snecked the door and paused to lock it
And plunge the key in some deep pocket.
Then as she tripped demurely down
The steep descent, the little town
Spread wider till its sprawling street
Enclosed her and her footfalls beat
On hard stone pavement, and she felt
Those throbbing ecstasies that melt

Through heart and mind, as, happy, free,
Her small, prim personality
Merged into the seething strife
Of auction-marts and city life.

She visits the Bootmaker,

Serenely down the busy stream
Miss Thompson floated in a dream.
Now, hovering bee-like, she would stop
Entranced before some tempting shop,
Getting in people's way and prying
At things she never thought of buying:
Now wafted on without an aim:
Until in course of time she came
To Watson's bootshop. Long she pries
At boots and shoes of every size,
Brown football-boots with bar and stud
For boys that scuffle in the mud,
And dancing-pumps with pointed toes
Glassy as jet, and dull black bows;
Slim ladies' shoes with two-inch heel
And sprinkled beads of gold and steel—
"How anyone can wear such things!"
On either side the doorway springs
(As in a tropic jungle loom
Masses of strange thick-petalled bloom
And fruits misshapen) fold on fold
A growth of sandshoes rubber-soled,
Clambering the door-posts, branching, spawning,
Their barbarous bunches like an awning
Over the windows and the doors.
But, framed among the other stores,
Something has caught Miss Thompson's eye
(O worldliness! O vanity!),
A pair of slippers—scarlet plush.

Miss Thompson feels a conscious blush
Suffuse her face, as though her thought
Had ventured further than it ought.
But O that colour's rapturous singing
And the answer in her lone heart ringing!
She turns (O Guardian Angels, stop her
From doing anything improper!)
She turns; and see, she stoops and bungles
In through the sandshoes' hanging jungles,
Away from light and common sense,
Into the shop dim-lit and dense
With smells of polish and tanned hide.

Soon from a dark recess inside   *Mrs. Watson.*
Fat Mrs. Watson comes slip-slop
To mind the business of the shop.
She walks flat-footed with a roll—
A serviceable, homely soul,
With kindly, ugly face like dough,
Hair dull and colourless as tow.
A huge Scotch-pebble fills the space
Between her bosom and her face.
One sees her making beds all day.
Miss Thompson lets her say her say
" So chilly for the time of year.
It's ages since we saw you here."
Then, heart a-flutter, speech precise,
Describes the shoes and asks the price.
" Them, Miss? Ah, them is six-and-nine."
Miss Thompson shudders down the spine
(Dream of impossible romance).
She eyes them with a wistful glance,
Torn between good and evil. Yes,   *Wrestles with a*
For half-a-minute and no less   *Temptation;*

<small>And is Saved;</small>

Miss Thompson strives with seven devils,
Then, soaring over earthly levels,
Turns from the shoes with lingering touch—
" Ah, six-and-nine is far too much.
Sorry to trouble you. Good day ! "

<small>She visits the fishmonger,</small>

A little further down the way
Stands Miles's fish-shop, whence is shed
So strong a smell of fishes dead
That people of a subtler sense
Hold their breath and hurry thence.
Miss Thompson hovers there and gazes :
Her housewife's knowing eye appraises
Salt and fresh, severely cons
Kippers bright as tarnished bronze :
Great cods disposed upon the sill
Chilly and wet, with gaping gill,
Flat head, glazed eye, and mute, uncouth,
Shapeless, wan, old-woman's mouth.
Next a row of soles and plaice
With querulous and twisted face,
And red-eyed bloaters, golden-grey ;
Smoked haddocks ranked in neat array ;
A group of smelts that take the light
Like slips of rainbow, pearly bright ;
Silver trout with rosy spots,
And coral shrimps with keen black dots
For eyes, and hard and jointed sheath
And crisp tails curving underneath.
But there upon the sanded floor,
More wonderful in all that store
Than anything on slab or shelf,
Stood Miles, the fishmonger, himself.

Foursquare he stood and filled the place. *Mr. Miles.*
His huge hands and his jolly face
Were red. He had a mouth to quaff
Pint after pint : a sounding laugh,
But wheezy at the end, and oft
His eyes bulged outwards and he coughed.
Aproned he stood from chin to toe.
The apron's vertical long flow
Warped grandly outwards to display
His hale, round belly hung midway,
Whose apex was securely bound
With apron-strings wrapped round and round.
Outside, Miss Thompson, small and staid,
Felt, as she always felt, afraid
Of this huge man who laughed so loud
And drew the notice of the crowd.
Awhile she paused in timid thought,
Then promptly hurried in and bought
" Two kippers, please. Yes, lovely weather."
" Two kippers ? Sixpence altogether : "
And in her basket laid the pair
Wrapped face to face in newspaper.

Then on she went, as one half blind, *Relapses into Temptation;*
For things were stirring in her mind :
Then turned about with fixed intent
And, heading for the bootshop, went
Straight in and bought the scarlet slippers *And Falls.*
And popped them in beside the kippers.

So much for that. From there she tacked, *She visits the Chemist,*
Still flushed by this decisive act,
Westward, and came without a stop
To Mr. Wren the chemist's shop,

And stood awhile outside to see
The tall big-bellied bottles three—
Red, blue, and emerald, richly bright
Each with its burning core of light.
The bell chimed as she pushed the door.
Spotless the oilcloth on the floor,
Limpid as water each glass case,
Each thing precisely in its place.
Rows of small drawers, black-lettered each
With curious words of foreign speech,
Ranked high above the other ware.
The old strange fragrance filled the air,
A fragrance like the garden pink,
But tinged with vague medicinal stink
Of camphor, soap, new sponges, blent
With chloroform and violet scent.

Mr. Wren.

And Wren the Chemist, tall and spare
Stood gaunt behind his counter there.
Quiet and very wise he seemed,
With skull-like face, bald head that gleamed:
Through spectacles his eyes looked kind.
He wore a pencil tucked behind
His ear. And never he mistakes
The wildest signs the doctor makes
Prescribing drugs. Brown paper, string,
He will not use for any thing,
But all in neat white parcels packs
And sticks them up with sealing-wax.
Miss Thompson bowed and blushed, and then
Undoubting bought of Mr. Wren,
Being free from modern scepticism,
A bottle for her rheumatism:
Also some peppermints to take

In case of wind ; an oval cake
Of scented soap ; a penny square
Of pungent naphthaline to scare
The moth. And after Wren had wrapped
And sealed the lot, Miss Thompson clapped
Them in beside the fish and shoes :
" Good day," she says, and off she goes.

Beelike Miss Thompson, whither next ? *Is Led Away by the Pleasures of the Town,*
Outside, you pause awhile, perplext,
Your bearings lost. Then all comes back
And round she wheels, hot on the track
Of Giles the Grocer : and from there *Such as Groceries and Millinery,*
To Emilie the Milliner,
There to be tempted by the sight
Of hats and blouses fiercely bright.
(O guard Miss Thompson, Powers that Be,
From Crudeness and Vulgarity.)

Still on from shop to shop she goes *And Other Allurements ;*
With sharp bird's-eye, enquiring nose,
Prying and peering, entering some,
Oblivious of the thought of home.
The town brimmed up with deep-blue haze,
But still she stayed to flit and gaze,
Her eyes ablur with rapturous sights,
Her small soul full of small delights,
Empty her purse, her basket filled.
The traffic in the town was stilled.
The clock struck six. Men thronged the inns. *But at length is Convinced of Indiscretion,*
Dear, dear, she should be home long since.

Then as she climbed the misty downs, *And Returns Home.*
The lamps were lighted in the town's

Small streets. She saw them star by star
Multiplying from afar :
Till, mapped beneath her, she could trace
Each street, and the wide square market-place
Sunk deeper and deeper as she went
Higher up the steep ascent.
And all that soul-uplifting stir
Step by step fell back from her,
The glory gone, the blossoming
Shrivelled, and she, a small, frail thing,
Carrying her laden basket. Till
Darkness and silence of the hill
Received her in their restful care
And stars came dropping through the air.

But loudly, sweetly sang the slippers
In the basket with the kippers ;
And loud and sweet the answering thrills
From her lone heart on the hills.

THE WISE MAN'S SONG

What is Space? A green bough, bright
In the sunshine of the Infinite,
And Time is but the curved wave's motion
In Eternity's smooth ocean.

Yet no wave can come to be
But from the dark womb of the sea,
And the sunlight is not known
Save by what it shines upon.

Never search the dim and vast.
All Eternity goes past
In a schoolboy's merry laughter,
And the Infinite is spanned
When girls go dancing hand in hand,
Between one step and the step after.

From Martin Secker's List

Collected Poems
 By Lord Alfred Douglas 7s. 6d. net
Collected Poems
 By J. E. Flecker 10s. net
Selected Poems
 By J. E. Flecker 3s. 6d. net
Country Sentiment
 By Robert Graves 5s. net
The Pier-Glass
 By Robert Graves 5s. net
The Village Wife's Lament
 By Maurice Hewlett 3s. 6d. net
Collected Poems
 By F. M. Hueffer 7s. 6d. net
New Poems
 By D. H. Lawrence 5s. net
Verses
 By Viola Meynell 2s. 6d. net
The Queen of China
 By Edward Shanks 6s. net

Number Five John Street
Adelphi

SELECTIONS FROM MODERN POETS

MADE BY

J. C. SQUIRE

F'cap 8vo. 488 pp. 5s. net

Martin Secker